Harry Lyman Koopman

Morrow-Songs

1880-1898

Harry Lyman Koopman

Morrow-Songs
1880-1898

ISBN/EAN: 9783744771627

Printed in Europe, USA, Canada, Australia, Japan

Cover: Foto ©Thomas Meinert / pixelio.de

More available books at **www.hansebooks.com**

MORROW-SONGS

1880–1898

BY

HARRY LYMAN KOOPMAN

BOSTON, MASS.
H. D. EVERETT, PUBLISHER
1898

DEDICATION

Inly beloved, ere my songs take flight,
Grant them, I pray, acceptance in thy sight,
Who art my morrow-tide with hope elate,
And courage to confront the coming fate;
Yet art my midday strength and equal mind,
Who daily faith renewest in humankind;
And art no less the solace and repose
That come with darkness at my labor's close.
Morning and noon and even, O my wife,
Unite in thee my perfect day of life.

CONTENTS

CONTENTS

CONTENTS

MORROW-SONGS

FREEDOM

VANISHED the tender gleams
  That my past illumed;
In a blaze of noon-bright beams
  Is their dawn consumed.

A vision blasting with light
  Thy features give. —
Have I looked with naked sight
  On Thee, and live?

Or who will credit my tale,
  If I speak Thee true?
But, chosen of Thee, can I fail?
  I will dare and do.

NOTE.

In the following poem the description of the cathedral adopts, for the outside, somewhat the lines of the minster at Ulm with its single spire, among the spires of earth peerless in height and beauty; while the colors of the interior have been drawn from the more gorgeous cathedrals of the Ile-de-France, the cradle and the throne of Gothic architecture.

THE GOTHIC MINSTER

A SYMPHONY in stone; wherein all notes
  Wrung or upleaping from man's ruddy heart,
The low, the loud, the dull, the penetrating,
As up to heaven thronging they ascend,
In labyrinthean intertanglement,
O'ertaken in mid-harmony by form,
Stand bodied forth, eternized, visible.
No thin Memnonian murmur, faintly heard
At dawn or dusk with glad or plaintive strain,
Here swells a chorus never still, a vast
Millennial antiphon absolved from sound,
Which thrills and thunders on the eye alone;
The music of the world-wide life of man,
Its hopes and fears and sins and sacrifices,
Rapt adoration, faith by deeds confirmed,
Jaw-dropt credulity, keen questioning,
Death-scorning courage daunted by the dark,
Love barred with hate, with grossness purity,
Red-slipping war, the hammering hum of peace,
Hand-clasping brotherhood and manliness,
The joy of handiwork, whose rest is toil,
The joy of breathing, moving, loving life,
Immortalized and eloquent in stone.

Stand here at night in storm, when, through the
    gloom,
The great bulk seems a wall across the world,
Uprising jagged to the very sky,
And you could deem a hornèd Alp, rebellious
Against the encircling conclave of his peers,
Had by their doom been banished here to dwell,
With all his fretting pines and pinnacles.
But let the moon break forth, and through swift scud
Flicker and float upon these carven walls,
The mountain vanishes, and in its place
A structure gleams without a stain of earth,
A temple heaven-descended, or, as if
A convoy of blest angels chorusing,
As back to heaven they bore a saint's white soul,
Had ravished so the moonlight with their song,
That, where their notes fell, there the beams, trans-
    formed,
Had stood upstriving, and, as rose the hymn,
So rose the silver fane, until the sound
Was muffled by the stars; while far below,
Though far aloft to men, the snowy cross
Hung yearning for that vanished melody.
But stand before the minster when high noon
Throws its revealing light on tower and wall,
The airy structure hardens into stone;
Not all forgetful of the mountain form
It wore in darkness, nor the winged grace

6

THE GOTHIC MINSTER

And lightness of that moony masonry;
Yet plainly work of man, man at his best,
Highest aspiring and most self-forgetful,
Therefore most self-revealing.   Then, what self?
The genius of what master intellect
Shines here by baser hands wrought visibly?
No mighty genius, and no baser hands,
But common lives by faith and art exalted; —
Such workmen reared these walls, and carved these
    spires,
And shot yon shaft of beauty into air
Till the eye aches that follows, and the heart
Feels itself snatched from earth and swept on high,
As by the current of a soaring flame.

If then the greatness was not theirs that wrought,
What mastering motive so informed their lives
As through such lowly means to win expression?
Religion 't was, and art its ministrant,
The records answer; but the question comes,
If unto them the word "religion" spake
As in our ears to-day.   In every age
Bears not the word its new significance,
Or meanings manifold, though under all
Abide the root and spring of all religion,
The loneliness and longing of the soul
Orphaned of its ideal?   The eye within
Beholds an image of perfection,

7

But in the outer and embodied world
Sees only crudeness, failure, death, decay;
No circle round, no angle true, no life
But inly bears the seeds of its own death;
The redeless riddle of the universe:
The rain descending on the evil man
As on the good, and on the good as oft
The hail and lightning; nothing justified
Within the span of life; the heart awarding
Men's lot by merit, and aggrieved to find
That force on earth usurps the place of right;
Nor satisfied that with the ages' lapse
Wrong slowly is made right, if this man's hurt
Is never healed, nor that man's pride put down.
The heart has vision in its inmost shrine
Of love illimitable, its native air,
Its birthplace and its bourne; but sees on earth
Man's hand against his brother, hate and greed
Making the world a shambles, or a den
Of famine and of torture; yea! the lesson,
Learned after centuries, that 't is thriftier
To coin a brother's heart's-blood, drop by drop,
Than spill it wastefully by the swift sword.

But heart and mind refuse to answer no
To the enigma of the universe.
Though earth and air and sea and human life,
With all their voices, howl a negative,

THE GOTHIC MINSTER

Deep in the soul resounds eternal yea.
Therefore the soul back on itself returns,
And through itself, as though a glass, beholds
The infinite brought down to human ken,
The dateless, boundless, beauty, goodness, truth.
But not in all its hours can the soul scale
Those dizzy heights of contemplation,
Descend those depths and breathe with mortal
    breath ;
Nor have all souls that strength to climb and dive.
So, that the blind might share the seer's sight,
And that the seer in his hours of gloom
Might not forget the vision wonderful,
Men wrought them symbols that should reproduce
The shadowed glory, as the picture's lines
Recall the absent loved one.   Yea, they strove
By strong suggestions so to realize
The world unseen, that o'er the symbol seen
The unseen through the parted heaven should burst.
Many the symbols that in many lands
Throughout the ages have moved human hearts
With heavenly persuasion ; but with some
An age, a race, drank all the meaning dry,
And left a rocky channel to our thirst.
Yet other symbols spake to all men's hearts
And speak to after ages.   Such are those
Vast emblems of the life of man in God
And of God's life with men, that, long perfecting,

MORROW-SONGS

After the opening of the new millennium
For half a thousand years ceased not to break
Flower-like on Europe's air, as if the rocks
Had risen in worship, and the forest aisles
Had joined them in uplifted adoration.

For him who from our naked shore brings eyes
Of unblest innocence, which never saw
Beauty in stone nor vaulted awfulness,
Yet brings a heart that thrills to grace and gloom
What ravishment awaits !   On him unwarned,
In all their beauty and their fragrance, burst
These fadeless blossoms of the centuries.
Upon his ears not dulled by frequency
The mighty chords of these vast instruments
Shatter full diapason.   O'er his soul
The symbol once again breaks up the depths
Of the unfathomed blue to melt beneath
The glory of the infinite descending.
Man's life in God, so mounts the soaring pile ;
Foundations vast and broad laid far below
In sunless depths of unseen sacrifice ;
The walls arising, buttressed all about
With rallying support ; oft scarcely more
Than buttresses, so precious is the room
For inward light ; then shrinking in the roof,
Then, as if taking heart, once more the walls
Rise heavenward, many-windowed, through a maze

10

THE GOTHIC MINSTER

Of buttresses that spring to meet the lower,
Then leap in upward flame for very joy
Of help received and given ; while, through all
The length and breadth of the vast edifice,
No line but upward strives, no stone but lifts,
No smallest spire or finial but stands
On tiptoe to ascend.   But not so broad
Can mount the highest life.   The roof shuts in ;
And all the upward impulse of the pile
Narrows into the tower, which climbs and climbs,
But though so far from earth not yet finds heaven ;
Too earthly still, it throws more weight away ;
A flying cloud is scarce so airy now ;
But still the vision waits, and still the spire,
Now narrowed to a staff, holds on its aim,
Will not give o'er until the blessing fall ;
And see, the stone begins to bud with hope ;
Swifter the spire shoots up, then suddenly
Stops, and in the rose-cross blossoms forth
For rapture of the beatific vision.

So finds the life of man its rest in God,
After long toil, repose ; long warfare, peace.
Where finds it ?   Yonder, never here on earth,
The upward-pointing answers.   Finds what life ?
The heart still urges, and for answer given
Receives the beckoning of the sculptured portal.
With heart upturned and chastened soul go in ;

MORROW-SONGS

The world shuts down behind, and thou art left
Alone in presence of the ineffable.
The very light is not the light of day ;
For here the sun shines not, but living light
With its effulgence glorifies the air,
As if the rainbow's promise filled the world.
All vistas end in light ; past range on range
Of columns down the illimitable aisle
A glory shuts the vision ; while, above,
From gloom to splendor soar the vaulted heights.
To right, to left, the air is dyed with hues,
Rich, darkling, solemnly magnificent,
Like the deep organ tones that from aloft
Roll under the huge vaults, and die away
Along the lessening arches dim and far.
Hours here are ages ; time has oped his hand
And let the soul fly free ; the bounds of space
Hem its light wings no longer.   Where and when
Have lost their meaning to the mind entranced.
Yea, self itself is lost ; the weary soul,
After long flight, within the bosom rests
Of the eternal, as the spray-flung drop
Sinks back in ocean's immensity.

What shall bring back the soul to earthly life,
After such heavenly ravishment, lest it faint,
Being clothed upon with flesh, in that fine air ?
Beauty : which links the human and divine,

THE GOTHIC MINSTER

And lures the soul on heavenly meads astray
Down its bright pathways to humanity.
At last the eye begins with separate sight
To mark what wholly had but dazzled it.
The mind, by suddenness of the splendor stunned,
Now step by step and slowly traverses
The strange new world revealed; and finds it all
Not wholly new or strange.   The forms are here
That build the forest's awe, the cavern's dread,
And, more familiar still, the lowlier shapes
Of leaf and bud and flower, with vines that cling
And coil and twine and creep and nestle or climb;
All wrought with faithfulness that comes alone
To love, a love that cherishes the life,
Not merely the dead forms.   Then the mind's eye
Pictures the workman of that elder time
On Sunday with his children wandering
In wood and field, and noting curve and poise
Of flower and leaf and stem, while constantly
His children bring him brighter, sweeter blooms
For his approval.   Wearying at last,
They lighten with their songs the homeward way.
No man might hope to see the pile complete,
But yet his daily, weekly, yearly task
He wrought and finished, and in doing it
Found happiness.   Toil might his body tire,
But in his heart was never any wish
Save to renew his task with the new day;

So much he loved the work.   His toil to him
Was recreation, for it ministered
To mind and heart; in it his thought and will
Wrought their creative impulse, and he knew
The artist's joy, finding in art his life.

Men build no more cathedrals; — walls may rise,
With tower and window, and be consecrate
To the old purpose, but the soul is fled.
Small need the cause to question.   Who toils now
For love of art, with high creative joy?
No laborer.   Then in vain the master plans,
Or, rather, vain his plan, and void of soul.
Art knows no sundering of the hand and brain;
The two as one must labor, for in art
The greater sinks or rises with the less.
But, given the art, should we be able still
To lift such clouds of incense to the sky,
By marble less than faith made permanent?
The question holds its answer; for the faith
That bade these mountains be removed and wrought
Into new shapes of heavenlier loveliness
Is dead on earth, never to live again.
That faith is dead; light slew it; when men came
To know the world they live in, and themselves,
The faith that pointed them away from earth,
And bade them scorn and flee it, could not live.
With all the beauty and the nameless charm

THE GOTHIC MINSTER

And soothing of the soul and inspiration
And lessons, which their monuments retain,
The old beliefs of twilight, when day dawned,
Must needs grow thin and vanish like the night.
That faith is dead which made the earth a waste,
And man's life but a desert pilgrimage
O'er burning sands and flinty shards to find
Beyond its bounds a Paradise and rest.
That faith is dead which in the body saw
Only the spirit's prison, a house of sin,
To be escaped from, not indwelt with joy.
That faith is dead, with its black pessimism,
Which deemed this world the devil's world, and then,
That men might not die wholly in despair,
Fashioned a heaven for earth's apology.
That faith is dead, but its dark influence
Yet shadows us.   Now men discern at last
That whatsoever other lives and worlds
Within the unrevealed may wait for man,
Yet is this earth his home, the theatre,
Where, and not elsewhere, he must play his part ;—
So much is sure ; the rest is dread or hope ; —
How do men greet this knowledge ?   How for this
Has the old faith prepared them ?   Alas ! the heart,
In the long years wherein the mind has grown
To stature and strength of manhood, has been fed
On childish food, and in its weakliness
Staggers beneath the burden.   Some men therefore

Rush out of life, preferring any change,
Or nothingness itself, to life on earth.
Others, like wolves, against their fellows turn
And rend the weak and wounded, feasting on them.
Others, retreating to the charnel house
Of the dead faith, pretend that life is there.
But most men to themselves seem aimlessly
Hurrying to and fro and finding naught.

Yet, unto one who from the minster tower
Looks down along the centuries to the ground,
They seem to move in common; and the sight
Awakes within his heart a faith, to which
That elder faith was childish fantasy.
What the new life shall be toward which men move
No tongue can tell, for it no eye hath seen;
But whence they move is clear; therefore in part
The whither we may guess.   Away from hate,
Away from violence, men slowly draw,
And leave behind the huddling fear of force,
Which sinks in mass the individual,
And leave the vapors of world-ignorance,
Whereon man saw his morning shadow thrown,
And fell before its vastness, worshiping;
And leave with every lie some love of lies.
Hence deem we kindliness and brotherhood,
Respect for others born of self-respect,
And bold research in room of cringing awe,

THE GOTHIC MINSTER

Shall have their home in that new world men seek;
And though on earth they seek it, is it less
Than that celestial city which John saw
Descending out of heaven unto men,
Wherein was no defilement, no more curse,
Abomination, lie in love or deed,
Sorrow nor crying more, nor any night,
But blessedness and healing of the nations?
No temple stood therein; for in that world
Symbol in sight is lost.   There the eternal
Is manifest in full-flowered human life,
Which finds itself in the eternal found.
More we cannot discern, and if we saw
We could but misinterpret; but no doubt
That newer life will bring its new ideals,
New character, new conduct, new religion;
Which if revealed to us were meaningless
Or profanation.   Let us be content
With what the far height of the tower unfolds
Of man's divine progression.

               If, in times
When all things change, our hearts distrust and
    doubt,
Turn we to where the Gothic minster lifts
Its cross above the ages, and there learn
How through the old life's death the new is born:
A thousand years one order ruled the world,

One form for every temple, wrought upon
The hard lines of the Roman's hall of state.
It added first the symbol of the cross,
Then arched the mighty dome of heaven's peace;
The walls reached out their level length, and stood
In strength a bulwark against all the world;
While, like a lower firmament, the roof,
Expansive, low, benignly sheltering,
Shut out the world above from that beneath;
On every window pressed the rounded arch,
And all was strong and stable and secure.
At last, with change of times, the order changed:
The windows robbed the wall's supremacy,
Grown wider, yet aspiring far aloft
In slender shafts that broke the restful lines
Of level, broken further by supports
To prop the weakened sides.   The roof, upheaved
As by a strong convulsion, cleft the air
A wedge, no more a shelter.   Losing power
To lift great domes in air, men reared instead
Dizzy and toppling spires.   Even the round
Of the strong arch was broken, and the whole,
To hide its death, was draped with carven flowers.
So, when at Amiens change had wrought its worst,
In the completed pile no trace was left
Of the old meaning; and, to eyes that saw
After the ancient order, seemed alone
Ruin, where we behold the full-blown rose

THE GOTHIC MINSTER

Of Gothic beauty, and discern therein
Meanings that more transcend what they displaced
Than those the coldness of the Roman hall.
The elder order built with lifeless weight
Of stone on stone against the outer light;
With all its strength it perished; but the new
Abides, which builds with life and light and love.

THE CONQUEROR *

A KNIGHT withouten golden spurs,
  Or shield or plumy crest,
Or axe or brand to take in hand,
    Or lance to lay in rest;

A knight for whom no champing steed
    Impatient paws the ground;
By squire unfollowed, and by rede
    Of minstrel unrenowned;

No lordly mould of brow or limb,
    Nor eye's imperial ken,
Nor grace of speech distinguish him
    Above his fellow-men;

* From this point onward the poems are arranged in order of time.

MORROW-SONGS

And they that see him day by day,
    With eyes of outward sight,
Have never guessed he rideth quest
    Or hath been dubbed a knight.

But weary eye and weary arm
    And heart world-overworn
Bespeak how near hope lies to fear,
    While blows yet must be borne.

*   *   *   *   *

Oh! couldst thou deem that at the last
    Thy God would leave thee so?
Hark to the heavenly trumpet blast,
    The death-knell of thy foe!

Mankind at length are open-eyed,
    And, all along the sky,
Behold their beacon-fires that wide
    Proclaim thy victory.

For only Truth can triumph long,
    And they that work its will
Then conquer most when foemen boast
    Their bodies slain and still.

JOHN BROWN

THE sea-bound landsman, looking back to shore,
    Now learns what land is highest;— not the ring
  Of hills that erewhile shut out everything
Beyond them from him ; these are seen no more ;
Nor yet the loftier heights that, from the lower,
    He saw far inland, blue, and, worshiping,
    Believed they touched the sky ; the gull's white
        wing
Long since flashed o'er them sunk in the sea-floor.
These were but uplands hiding the true height,
    Which looms above them as they sink, and rears
Its greatness ever greater on the sight.
    So thou, across the widening sea of years,
Aye risest great, as on through gloom and bright
    Our tossing bark of Progress sunward steers.

THE SOWERS

THERE went three sowers forth to sow,
    In the shining days when the earth was young ;
One scarfed with the dawning-light did go,
    For out of the east his steps had sprung ;
And seeds of knowledge he bore in his hand
To scatter broadcast over the land.

21

MORROW-SONGS

Another came from the midday heat,
    And seeds of beauty he sowed afar;
Resplendent vapors rolled at his feet,
    And his brows were bright as the sun-lands are;
To the lands of midnight away he strode,
And the dawn and the gloaming beneath him glowed.

The third came out of the star-lit north,
    With the rush of winds and of waters he came;
And seeds of duty he scattered forth,
    Far-flung like the northern dayspring's flame;
Till dale and hillside, from sea to sea,
Were bright with the bloom of his husbandry.

But that was ages and ages gone,
    The sowers are now at rest from their toil;
The threefold harvest is drawing on,
    For the dry stalks clash o'er a withered soil.
Already the reapers throng amain
With shining sickles among the grain.

For out of the west the reapers pour
    To reap the harvest the three have sown,
To bind the sheaves for the threshing-floor,
    Where history's fruit shall at last be shown;
And beauty, knowledge, and duty then
Shall yield their bread for the life of men.

22

PROGRESS

ENLARGED horizons, ampler life, are gains
Less than their proof mankind still onward
strains.

REFORM

HALT! hear ye not the cry,
That voice not loud nor high,
But a mighty undertone,
From the four winds of heaven blown?
Hark! ye can hear it now,
The sound men heard of yore,
Making the tyrant bow,
And crumbling sceptre and throne.
Hark to the gathering roar,
And flee from the coming storm.
Reform, reform, reform!

What! an ye will not hear,
Look the horizon round,
See how the wroth clouds rear
Their blackness from the ground.
The blue sky shrivels in dread,
It is furled as a sail is furled;
There are fiery bolts to be sped,

23

For the vengeance waxeth warm,
For justice wakes on the world,
And woe to the guilty head.
Reform, reform, reform !

Nay, it is now too late !
Ye heed, but we cannot wait ;
The tempest has drawn too nigh ;
Its threaded lightnings ply,
And a fiery shroud they weave.
Fools, ye would not believe,
Ye doubted, and ye must die.
Ye vanish, and where ye stood
The hosts of the upright swarm,
Their battle-cry made good :
Reform, reform, reform !

THE THINKER

A PURBLIND mole bored underneath a stone,
A castle's corner-stone.   Then came a storm
And swept the stronghold to the ground, and men
Wondered a wind should have such power to smite.

HEAVEN

OUT of the world of illusion into the world of
truth,
From the world of change and dying to the world
of fadeless youth;
Where the eye of man unclouded shall look on
things that are,
And the heart of man unwithered be free from sor-
row and care,
And the life of man, unfettered by bonds of time
and space,
Shall bloom as a god's, unsleeping, yea, lit by
God's own face.
O Father, 't is that fair kingdom Thy hands have
wrought for men;
From Thee was their beginning, to Thee they re-
turn again.

But forget not, O heart anhungered, that now,
and here on the earth,
Mayst thou dwell in that heavenly city, mayst
thou see with the soul's new birth;
For whoso liveth and striveth in service of truth
and of love,
To him yieldeth earth already the blessings prom-
ised above.

LIFE

LIFE is a passage o'er a stream
  That bridge nor ferry owns;
Which we must cross, in gloom or gleam,
  On slippery stepping-stones.

RECOGNITION

AT twenty, " Dreamer," pitying neighbors said;
  At thirty, " Fool," the harsher title came;
  At forty, " Crank," men sneered with scorn and
    blame;
But still the genius toiled with unbowed head,
Wide sowing seed that none saw harvested,
  Till, by and by, at fifty, some cried " Shame!
  Respect at least is due a noble aim."
So called him " Mister " guardedly instead.
At sixty, one must harvest, wheat or chaff;
  And now 't was " the Distinguished " that he
    heard.
At seventy, fields are reaped, the winners laugh;
  And he had won; " the Great " was now men's
    word.
At eighty, they inscribed ' His fame folds in
This orb o' the earth.' Yea, who but dreamers win?

26

INDIGNATION

SHOCK old proprieties, cross local forms,—
How Indignation in a moment storms!
Lie, cheat, bribe, steal, thrust orphans out of doors,—
And Indignation in its arm-chair snores.

TEMPTATION

HER his divine scorn back to virtue won;
He by his second temptress was undone.

HOME *

HAIL, Mother of us all! from sea and shore
Thy children gather round thy knees once
more;
The faithful ones that never left thy side,
And they whose feet have wandered far and wide.
How dear these love thee, in thy sheltering nest,
Thy happier children, all their lives attest;
But they no less that under alien skies
In tearful memory mark thy homes arise.

* Read at the centennial celebration of the town of Freeport, Maine,
July fourth, 1889.

MORROW-SONGS

The fevered sailor on the Spanish Main
Sees in thy springs his boyhood's face again.
The homeless toiler 'mid the city's roar
In midnight watches visits thee once more,
Retraces every step his childhood trod,
And in his garret plucks thy goldenrod,
Or breathes the fragrance of the mayflower meek
One moment that blots out the city's reek;
And even those whose sun sets in the sea
Prairie and mountain cannot part from thee.
Serener, softer skies may arch above,
Thy children yield them a divided love.
Let now the homage all have paid so long
In grateful silence, voice itself in song,
While flock thy nurselings from the ends of earth
To greet thee on thy second century's birth.

O Mother Town, thy children love thee well,—
For what they love thee let our praises tell.
Thy skies we love, whether they laugh with blue,
Or frown with clouds the tempest hurtles through;
For sheltering still their vastness o'er thee bends,
A shield whose dome from hill to sea extends.
Thy hills we love, whose granite ridges show
Westward the summits of late-lingering snow;
Themselves to eastward many a watery mile
The sailor's promise of his children's smile.
How oft, far inland, gray-beard sons of thine,

HOME

Catching the scent of rope or tarry twine,
Have felt the odor in a flash restore
Thy river-port, the shipyards on the shore!
Again the mallets ply their clattering din,
The tackles chirp, the screeching planes join in,
While from the sooty cauldron spreads afar
The wholesome fragrance of the boiling tar.
They see the boys with mimic boats at play,
The white sails flashing in the outer bay,
With wooded islands peeping still beyond,
Enchanted isles, the gates of " faery lond."
Yea, dear is Haraseket's blue expanse ;
Dear also every brooklet's foamy dance,
Dusking and dimpling down the wooded hills,
Where streaming moss its frolic tinkle stills.
We love thy spruces, hemlocks, and thy firs,
Cross-bearing, but unwearied worshipers ;
Thy maples, Autumn's chariot of fire,
Thy royal elms that robed in gold expire ; .
And even the wild roses by the way
Our memories cherish many a thorny day.

The ships that make thy name no longer strange
Wherever commerce and its ventures range,
These love we ; but our warmer love arouse
The manly hearts that urge their frothing prows ;
Nor these alone, but all the sons of toil
That reap God's harvests in the wave or soil.

Such are earth's noblemen. In after-time,
When Right shall reckon idleness a crime,
Who earns not shall not eat, nor any knave
Shall make by law his fellow-man his slave;
For God's great granary of earth shall be
No longer fenced, but, as the winds are, free.
What sturdy sons thy lap hath given to fame
Where learning builds, let Rochester proclaim.
What inspiration from thy fields hath sprung
To lend art hues and piety a tongue,—
Hark to the champion of the Rising Faith,
Hear what Œnone's pictured beauty saith!

Our pulses leap, we glow with filial pride,
Yet is unspoken more than all beside.
O brave young souls who at your country's call
Gave life itself, and deemed the offering small,
If you we name not this memorial day
May tyrants filch our liberties away.
Ah no! your fame is blazoned on the sky;
Your lives ye lost to find eternally.
And oh! the sainted, nameless, unforgot
Sweet souls that live, though now we see them not,
Whose lives were love to daily duty set,
Whose prayers, we know, are not all answered yet,
Whose memories blossom o'er their dust entombed,
As Aaron's rod, long dead, to fragrance bloomed.
'T is these that teach us what of thine we prize,—

HOME

Not chiefly nature's boon of fields and skies,
Which other climes in richer store extend,
Unclouded heavens, and harvests without end,
Where, free from blight of frost and suns that sear,
Perpetual spring leads round the laughing year.
Such blessings here we need not, satisfied
With one chief good that beggars all beside.
For here, our lives, though wide they learn to roam,
Find last, as first, and only here, the Home.

Resting on earth, but leading up to heaven,
Like Bethel's ladder, home to man was given.
First ray of love in self's benighted life,
The care for other self in maid and wife ;
Then pity quickened for the crying child,
Last, duty ; and the man that roamed the wild,
Chief brute in cunning, but with death his goal,
Breathed on by God became a living soul.
O childhood's home, what memories haunt thy
        name !
Of prayers the mother taught when twilight came,
Her kiss that cheered the urchin's steps to school,
The father's praise where silence was the rule,
The mysteries of morning, noon, and night,
Transfigured all by love's celestial light,
When all the world was new, and all was good,
And midmost of the world the household stood.
Wide now the world has grown, but not so wide

As oft the gulf that parts men side by side.
Though petty seem the joys which then we knew,
They filled our hearts, as now what triumphs do?
Yea, toil itself was pleasure, for the work
Was done in love, and not as hirelings shirk.
Here beauty wrought, revealing heaven's design
That only service can make life divine;
And well had wrought if never stranger's gaze
Had waked the great world's chorus of its praise.
Here sturdy yeomen, toiling without shame,
Amassed the riches of an honest name,
And taught their sons to walk where they had trod,
Speak truth, and love their country and their God.

Beloved town, with gladness we discern
How fortune smiles on thee at every turn,
And trust that all its present favor brings
Is but the earnest of still goodlier things;
Yet on this day, the fulness of thy years,
One word the poet brings not free from fears.
Dear Home Town, let men ever call thee so;
Guard well the fount from which thy virtues flow.
Only thy homes can rear thee manly sons
And daughters gentle, as thine earlier ones.
Only thy homes, when dawns this day again,
Can bring thee love like ours from future men.
O Land of Homes, amid the storms to fall,
No fear be thine if thou hast homes for all.

HOME

Assured of this, let drowning rains descend,
And all the winds their wrath against thee bend;
The fleeting sands may shift with every shock,
Not thou, for thou art founded on a rock.
O Mother Earth, then blooms thy perfect flower
Only when perfect homes prepare the hour;
The perfect flower of Earth, the perfect pair,
Whose Eden yet awaits them everywhere!

As Europe's vast cathedrals, piled in stone,
Displaced the trees that on their sites had grown,
Yet in their aisles and arches but renewed
The living outlines of the primal wood,
Even so our dreams of human life at best,—
Mankind restored, its demons dispossessed,
Where labor waits on health and joy and truth,
And beauty finds in love eternal youth,—
Our visions, as they shape themselves in air,
And clearer grow, familiar faces wear,
Till, when at last their structure rounds to view,
'T is only the old home-life builded new.

THE OUTLOOK

BY A CONSERVATIVE

WHEN I was young I sighed for fame,
 And burned the midnight oil;
But, now I 'm old, my blood is tame,
I sit and nurse the sea-coal's flame,
 And read how others toil.

Here Henry George, for all he 's worth,
 Proclaims his one taxation,
Crusading to set free the earth,
And make the loafer, rich from birth,
 Dismount his poor relation.

There Bellamy, another crank,
 Fiction with fact would mingle;
He sees that men in file and rank,
Like oars arranged in tier and bank,
 Beat twice their number single.

And so the great industrial mob
 He 'd mold into an army,
And send it forth to kill and rob
Famine and Surfeit, which hobnob,
 While discontent grows barmy.

THE OUTLOOK

" Amen ! " cries Boston's Dawn of Bliss,
  " But don't be too paternal.
Fraternal the true watchword is.
Man in management to miss
  Were tyranny infernal."

Yonder Macready calls, whose cue
  Seems caught from sport, not killing,
" See how the players dare and do ;
What order, yet what ardor too !
  Because each part is willing."

He 'd have no man controlled by man,—
  Police or politician ;
For each will do the best he can,
Simply through fear of public ban,
  Or hope of recognition.

So *he* holds ; and this loose-hung state
  He calls ideal freedom ;
Where men may join or separate,
Live gods or beasts, in love or hate,
  As happiness shall lead 'em.

The poet Morris, oversea,
  Sick of civilization,
Dreams how England's wealth may be
Common wealth, and Britons free
  Even from education.

MORROW-SONGS

In Germany upstarts Mackay,
   The monarch self proclaiming,
Across the Storm a steadying cry,
A torch to lighten earth and sky,
   For equal freedom flaming.

" Bravo ! " shouts Tucker, looking up
   Above the Transatlantic.
" That 's Liberty ; that 's Proudhon's cup,
Whereof when nations learn to sup,
   Their greatness grows gigantic."

Last, Sullivan exclaims serene :
   " God bless you all, my hearties ! "
Deuce take them, I say, for I 've seen
Too much reform to care a bean
   For any of their parties.

I 'll wager if I had 'em here,
   Well fed, with none that know by,
Two fingers round a glass of beer,
Some good havanas lying near,
   They 'd give the crowd the go-by.

I 'd wager, yet I won't be sure ;
   I own I can't quite place them.
You 'd really think they love the poor,
Gold seems powerless to allure,
   Or honors to debase them.

THE OUTLOOK

'T was like this in the tiresome days
   We now call *ante-bellum*;
Garrison setting all ablaze,
And Beecher drowning Parker's brays,
   With Phillips to outyell 'em;

Whittier hounding us in rhyme,
   And Mrs. Stowe in fiction,
And Lowell with them keeping time,
But trying to disguise his crime
   Beneath the rabble's diction.

I promise these the self-same fate.
   Who now spouts abolition?
Just so you 'll see, if you but wait,
A time when fools no longer prate
   About the poor's condition.

APPRECIATION

WE crowned with thorns the living hero's brow;
   But see, we deck his grave with roses now.

Now! while the very stones from which he bled
Climb to a monument above his head.

THE PIONEER

HERE shall be smiling fields, where now the fell
　　And ravening wolf howls to his echoed howl;
　　Babies shall prattle where couched panthers
　　　　growl,
And lovers clip and coo in many a dell
Which now the savage wakes with midnight yell
　　To blood and flame and frenzied orgies foul.
　　Already light breaks in on bat and owl
O'er crashing trees.　The settler's axe aims well.

How desperate are beginnings!　But, at last,
　　Where one and then a hundred sadly wrought,
Throng, on a sudden, millions, and the past
　　Becomes heroic, with men's praises fraught.
Take my praise now, while still thy toils loom vast,
　　Lone outpost on the far frontier of thought.

THE HIGHER HARMONY

THE soul attuned to music of the spheres
　　Strikes often discords unto earthly ears.

NUMBERS

THE crowd is always on the side of truth ;
But commonly not long before the truth
Has in that special form become a lie.

THE HEAVENLY VISION

WHEN I am dead,
May this with truth be said,
On the rude stone that marks my lowly head,
That, spite of doubt and indecision,
In spite of weakness, lameness, blindness,
Heart's treachery and fate's unkindness,
Neglect of friends and scorn of foes,
Stark poverty and all its woes,
The body's ills that clog the mind
And the bold spirit bind,
Still through my earthly course I went,
*"Not disobedient
Unto the heavenly vision."*

MY WASHERWOMAN

I LIVE at the upper end of the street,
Where the ground is clean and the air is sweet,
But all I can see is a patch of sky,
And lawns and painted walls hard by.
My washerwoman lives at the end
Where street and people downward tend;
Where the air is full of sickly smells
And unkempt, squabbling children's yells;
But, all day long, from her dingy room,
She can look where earth's first mountains loom,
Beyond the broad and living lake,
Whose deeps the sunset splendors take.

She looks, but, ah! she cannot see,
So blinding is her poverty.
On pain and hunger, heat and frost,
The pomp of earth and sky is lost.

And I that haste the foul street through,
Envying her its wealth of view,
I know that if some ill desert
Should doom me to its noise and dirt,
The change would bring me loss, not gain,
Though hourly through my narrow pane

MY WASHERWOMAN

I saw those primal mountains rise,
As proudly peerless to the skies
As when adown their slopes of old
The parted waters wallowing rolled.

THE CHURCH PROGRESSIVE

THE Church advances; to each new position
   Man's marching spirit takes she hobbles fast,
Asserting shrill the hour she finds admission,
   That here she had her home through all the past.

FAILURE

YES, I succeeded, and have men's praise,
   And cannot escape it all my days.
My rival failed; — but every age
Shall thrill at the task he dared engage.

AFTER-LIFE

OF any other life than this we lead
   Now on the earth, nothing we know indeed;
But having this life, with its depth and range,
We know not whence, why seems another strange?

PRIESTCRAFT

AT Bruno's, Lessing's, Rousseau's monument
Priests glower aloof, their sullen spite to vent
Against those Sons of Dawn; for well they wot
When priestcraft dies its memory shall rot.

INHERITANCE

OUR godly fathers from the body stole
Comfort and beauty, to enrich the soul.
We, starved and stunted beneath rigor's frown,
Our souls in riot of the senses drown.

WHAT SHALL IT PROFIT?*

I.

AN EARLY PHYSICIAN

IF I lay waste and wither up with doubt
The confidence men have that fleshly ills
Are the invasion of a demon rout
    Whose fury charm or incantation stills,

* Suggested by Mr. Howells's poem in *Harper's Magazine* for February, 1891.

What shall it profit? for the sick are healed
  Oft with these if not by them, and shall I
Disturb men's faith, who have no help to yield,
  And leave the sick in their despair to cry?

II.

DOUBT

This profit is in doubt : until men fear
  They trust a lie, who will strive truth to find?
And what is faith but holding truth so dear
  We welcome doubt lest some lie lurk behind?
The truth abides; to halt with doubt perplexed
  Is the first step toward the truth's finding out.
Though one road fail, the next, or next, or next
  Shall lead to truth; for men are saved by doubt.

RICHES

FREEDOM the wood-nymph in a marish found
  A gilded asp, with glittering jeweled crest
And eyes of light. So gracefully it coiled,
With rainbow shimmer playing o'er its gold,
That Freedom, charmed, took up the lissome toy,
And let it coil about her sloping wrist,
And span her neck, and make its pliant nest

MORROW-SONGS

Among the soft curves of her youthful bosom.
For what should white-armed Freedom dream of ill!
Now lies she low, a purple-spotted corpse,
Poisoning the air, dead without sign of wound.
But those that nearer drew tell how they saw
A mark as of a tooth above the spot
Where once beat Freedom's heart.

PRUDENCE

INTO Truth's abandoned camp
Prudence mounts with martial tramp,
Celebrates a victory vast;
While the Truth, unseen, has passed
Onward in its desperate fight
With the cohorts of the Night.

EXTREMES

TRUTH is found in extremes; 't is only expe-
  dience, prudence,
Hug the mean, and call it truth, and their palter-
  ing, wisdom.
Both extremes may be true, but the mean, from its
  very nature,
Always has been, is, and must forever be untrue.

44

THE WAIL OF THE WOUNDED

THE WAIL OF THE WOUNDED

AFTER the Gettysburg fight,
   When war had ceased with the night,
Uncared-for the wounded lay,
Where they fell in the bloody fray,
Ten thousand on every side,
With the myriad more that died.
But oh! the chorus of pain
That rose from hillside and plain,
A vast, intermingled groan,
Shriek and howling and moan,
A volume that crowded the air,
Agony, anguish, despair,
In billows that rose and sank,
Till my soul became a blank,
By sympathy wrung too deep,
Escaping madness in sleep.

But often now I awake
With every limb a-quake,
And hair upstarting, wet,
While on my hearing yet
In torture shriek again
That landscape of wounded men.

OPPORTUNITY

THOR with his thunderous hammer smote the
    rock
Full nine and ninety times with bounding shock,
And still a mocking laugh the granite gave ;
Then Thor the thunderer slept within his grave.
I came, a stripling, dealt my puny stroke,
And into dust the stubborn boulder broke.

TRUTH

LIKE the dropping rain is truth,
    Which barren soil to foulness turns,
But life in fruitful soil reneweth,
    Till all the land with beauty burns.

M'CREADY *

HOW soon forgotten when we are gone !
    But here and there our lives bloom on
Perennial in faithful hearts,
Whose love recalls our played-out parts,

* Died June 16, 1890.

46

M'CREADY

And heaves a sigh o'er the broken thread,
And the roofless tower, and the path that led
To where the prairie's light and bloom
Began to break on the jungle's gloom.
For the spinning ceased, and the trowel fell,
And the pioneer, who had led so well
From the forest-depths to the clearing's verge,
Sank earthward, powerless to emerge.
But he left behind him a shining trail,
For others' guidance who shall not fail;
Who, pressing onward, shall easily win
To the gardens of beauty and enter in;
By thousands enter, till where he trod
They build an avenue, firm and broad;
At the side of which, near the forest's bound,
He lies in unremembering ground.
But the throngs that follow where first he went
Shall be his living monument.

STUMBLING-BLOCKS

LIFE'S greatest art, learned through its hardest
knocks,
Is to make stepping-stones of stumbling-blocks.

TWO CHARACTERIZATIONS

H. L. K.—Shelley's Adonais, 35a

AT last, long after these, a form appeared,
Some deemed it marsh-lamp, some a meteor
stray;
So low it moved that envy never bleared,
Nor hate nor malice stifled its thin ray;
Yet with love's rosy flame it burned alway,
Save wrath at wrong flushed it with vengeful red,
Or honor's hue, caught from the fount of day,
Or hope with gold of dawn was through it shed; —
Now pale with ruth and rue, it sought that stricken
head.

K. H. K.—Born January 1, 1892

To dare the right, though heaven denounce it sin,
To clasp the truth, though all men brand it lie,
To stand alone, until thy firmness win
The world to look and what thou seest descry,
To know thyself, and trust thine own clear eye
Against a multitude, greatly to love,
Greatly to be loved, void of jealousy,
And not even hate to hate; so live, and prove
The New Year's gift to earth its need has vision of.

INDIVIDUALISM

WHEN will all the world go right?
Never!— Right is infinite.
When will all the world go well?
That is different; I will tell:
When each man shall do no less
Nor more than mind his business,
And others would risk life and limb
Who dared to interfere with him;—
This whenever you shall see,
The world will then wag merrily.

NEW BIRTH

'TIS not reform the world wants,
A smoothing of this or that feature;
'T is not reform, but conversion,
A new, regenerate creature.

MASKS

THOUGHT is but the mask whereby
Life is hid, as word hides thought.
Ends the dance; and eye to eye
Soul and Life at last are brought.

WIT AND MADNESS

HIS sister, crazing, dreamed herself a queen,
And, after long years, in that fancy died;
Meanwhile, a poet, he, with brow serene,
Faced Life, its king;—as mad as she, men cried.

OPPRESSION

BROTHERS, ye still must suffering endure;—
'T is life's hard way its ills through pain to cure.
And cured shall yours be when your agony
Wrings you at last to ope your eyes and see.

THE BEGINNING OF CIVILIZATION

MAN outgrows like a garment and throws off
Law, which is custom armed; then custom
next,
That levelling instinct of the commonplace;
Last righteousness, which is the cramped cocoon
Wherein man's soul bred wings for flying free.
Then love shoots forth, fragrant and white, from lust,
As from its root in mud the water-lily.
Man's long, long term of barbarism ends,
Civilization and true life begin.

THE JEW *

THE Jew at his best and worst, Jesus and Shy-
lock stand; —
Galilee bred the one, the other a Christian land.

THE KING OF DARKNESS

IF I were the King of Darkness,
But one thing I should fear.—
I would toil as a liberal monarch
   To make my people freer;
I would take the tax off music,
   Words should be free as air;
All men should taste of the choicest,
   And revel in perfumes rare.
The softest of silk should clothe them,
   Their limbs should repose on down;
Naught should lack my approval,
   On no excess would I frown.
One only thing would I banish,
   And combat with all my might,—
The poisonous, blasphemous, impious,
   Nihilistic Light.

* The first line embodies a saying of my friend Robert Nicol.

MUSIC-LIFE

OVER the poet's eyes
   The clods are shoveled and trod.
Stifled in silence lies
   The seer who sang of God.

Wide o'er that voiceless mound
   The anthem's might outswells;
And I know — in the world of sound,
   Escaped, the spirit dwells.

RECREANT

HAD he died while his words of flame
   Were kindling every soul,
The world had written his name
   On its brightest hero-scroll.

But fate condemned him to live,
   And life his words to unsay;
Our idol we cannot forgive
   For crumbling to common clay.

But, trust me, 't is better so;
   No man should our homage own;
Our hearts should their faith bestow
   On Truth, and on Truth alone.

52

THE RULE OF MAMMON

L OADED with curses of men, and long for-
gotten of God;
This is the upas tree on its venom-blasted sod;
Loveless, lightless, foul, in its poison's reeking pall,
Befriended, known, but of Hate, where God smiles
over all.
The seasons cheer and strengthen, the morns their
life renew,
But here is naught that lives but the drip of mur-
der-dew,
And the ring of leperous greensward, whose oozy
death o'erpours,
Widening, widening, widening over earth's happy
shores;
And ever its charnel breath blackens the festered
sky,
And ever the ground that was made for men, who
have risen so high,
To grow from men into man, and, still ascending,
who knows?
To mount from man into godhead, ever the good
ground grows
But a breeding-place for devils, where they that
still have room
Choke their brothers backward into the stench and
gloom;

53

And both outdo the beasts in their clamorous claw-
    ing strife;
And still that circle of death spews over the green
    earth's life.
But, see, in the black above, the lightnings that
    probe to the clod!
An earthquake fumbles beneath.
                    No, not forgotten of God!

BIRTH

TO E. G. R.

FOR thee the mother's sacred joy
    That unto earth a man is born;
For him the love without alloy,—
    God's pledge,— unfailing even and morn.

HATE

THE hottest hate by vengeance fanned
    Burns not with instant wrath;
White molten iron will kiss thy hand,—
    But make it not thy bath!

TRUTH, PEACE, LOVE

TRUTH, PEACE, LOVE *

TRUTH

" WE buy the truth," cried Bunyan's pilgrim
     pair,
In that vile mart where truth ne'er entered in.
Here, amid industry's encroaching din,
Where traffic's tumult storms the trembling air,
What task is this ye deem than all more fair,
    What profit manifold look ye to win,
    What ore to smelt, what golden threads to spin,
What shop is this, what handiwork, what ware?

We build a mart to knowledge consecrate,
    Above whose door is writ " Let there be light."
On him that lacks our treasures freely wait,
    For eyes that see make not the sun less bright.
Free are our goods, yet is our profit great,
    For only truth preserves a nation's might.

PEACE

Of knowledge what shall be the earliest fruit?
    Oh! can ye doubt that first-fruit shall be peace?
    To earth's long agony bringing release,

* Read at the dedication of the Riverside Public Library.

Ending the trail of blood that from the brute
Hath ever followed man's advancing foot;
  To war and rumored war a last surcease.
  Desire of all the ages, blest increase
Of earth's blood-watered prayers, Peace we salute.

But canst thou dream these inoffensive ranks
  Have power to scatter war's embattled hosts?
That at their silent shock the navy's banks
  Of waiting death shall fade from earth's fair
    coasts?
Nay, 't is no dream. On Slaughter's bristling flanks
  Truth charges, and they melt like morning ghosts.

LOVE

For lo! a mighty spirit upon earth
  Descends, whereof Peace but forerunner fares;
  For Peace is naught, saving as it prepares
The whole round world a pathway for the mirth
And majesty that hasten to Love's birth;
  For Love shall reign wide as earth's wooing airs,
  Deep as man's heart, high as heaven's altar stairs,
Whose rule shall know no end, nor fulness dearth.

Love the fulfilment is of all the law,
  And all the æons of the travailing past;

56

TRUTH, PEACE, LOVE

Is in our hearts fulfilled, who here withdraw
    From ease and gain and strife, which heaven
        o'ercast,
That we may build this temple without flaw
    To Truth, to Peace, to Love, supreme and last.

JOHN HENRY MACKAY

WIDE through the world thou art driven
    By the spirit that lashes thy breast;
All life can give it hath given
    Thee freely, save only rest;

Rest, and the vision raising
    The vail over uttermost skies,—
The look that comes to me gazing
    Into my children's eyes.

ALONENESS

SIRIUS girt by worlds of light
    With lesser wonderment I mark
Than a glowworm in the forest's night,
    Where else is only dark.

COMRADE

" LET the dead bury their dead " quoth he ;
    And on he marched without more ado ;
Not a turn of the head, not a bend of the knee,
    For the comrade so tender and brave and true.

I care not; the Cause may linger now,
    While the stricken heart in its anguish cowers ;
I must kneel, and twine for that fair Greek brow
    A garland of dusty wayside flowers.

THE SATIRIST

NOT mine to draw the cloth-yard shaft
    From straining palm to thrilling ear ;
Then launch it through the monster's hulk,
    One thrust, from front to rear.

Mine is the Bushman's tiny bow,
    Whose wounds the foeman hardly feels ;
He laughs and lifts his hand to smite,
    Then, suddenly, he reels.

MIDWAY *

" Nel mezzo del cammin di nostra vita."

YOUTH for dreams, manhood for toil, age for
the dreams' fulfilling,
So runs the course of highest life, when all the gods
are willing.
So Dante dreamed and agonized, from sweet New
Life's romances,
Through strife and exile, to the sight that crowns
all human trances.
His face, that from the artist's brush had graced
the courts of Heaven,
Grew seared as if enswathed within his Malebolge's
levin;
And yet his heart passed on unbroke through Hell's
forlorn abysm,
Nor failed until it sank beneath the triune splen-
dor's chrysm.
So sweet Cervantes, sunrise-souled, with wounds
and fetters burdened,
Nursed in his heart the high resolve that fate, re-
pentant, guerdoned.
Before his smile the masquerade of folly, robed and
hollow,

* Written for the fifteenth anniversary of the class of 1880 in
Colby University.

Sank like the braying herds that felt the bright
    shafts of Apollo;
And, "one foot in the stirrup," still he wrought
    that all men wondered,
And Death, who bore his soul away, of half his
    booty plundered.
So Chaucer, touched by love's sweet pain to most
    melodious plaining,
Was doomed to con life's day-book lines of sordid
    loss and gaining;
But when at last for his account the great Task-
    master beckoned,
He smiled and held the world aloft with all its
    values reckoned.

Of all the darlings of the muse, foremost among
    her favored,
Blest with her full, peculiar love, that life-long
    never wavered,
Stand two supremely eminent: the one whom Flor-
    ence nourished,
The other round whose youthful steps the drama's
    fulness flourished.
But twice, O calm Urania, high-throned above our
    passions,
Twice only hast thou felt the pang that Death for
    mortals fashions:

MIDWAY

Once when beneath Ravenna's pines thy Dante's
    eyes were darkened,
And once when Milton, blind, alone, Death's icy
    footsteps hearkened.
A Samson straining at the posts his tugging could
    not level,
A captive 'neath the roof where Crime held high
    exultant revel;
Powerless to raze that Shrine of Sin, which mocked
    his might, victorious,
He turned, and high above it reared another shrine
    so glorious
That all the world with pilgrim feet now bends its
    worship thither,
Unmindful of the crumbling Shame, whose weeds
    untrodden wither;
So, to the dream of Milton's youth, his manhood's
    high ambition,
The gods accorded to his age to work a full frui-
    tion.
Men live who Hawthorne's morning saw by gloom
    of toil beclouded,
Yet witness how he bore his heart with no repining
    shrouded;
And when at length the darkness broke, lo! fame's
    serenest summit.
The height his youthful vision saw, his manhood's
    feet had clomb it.

O kindly friends within whose eyes the light of
    love arises,
Which once illumed our youthful blanks with glow
    of future prizes,
No trophies from the world we bring, save un-
    dimmed high endeavor,
Yet dare believe your toil, your faith, shall not be
    mocked forever.
Our dreams are dreamed; with eyesight purged of
    golden youth's illusion,
We see the world the maze it is of struggle and
    confusion.
No place for dreams! and yet we leave our castles
    high upbuilded,
Flushed with the rose of hope untried, with dawn's
    expectance gilded.
We turn, and deep in earth we delve, or swink in
    kiln and quarry,
Whereto? but that the world some day may see,
    and not be sorry,
Those airy outlines taking form in solid, shining
    marble,
A house of joy, where men may feast, while birds
    around it warble.
For History this proclaims, its flight world-wide
    through æons taking,
That naught abides save only dreams transmuted
    into waking.

ORIGINALITY

THE man who not yet seeth clear,
Confused by cries "Lo there!" "Lo
here!"
Can but proclaim another's sight.
But when he once hath seen aright,
Pierced to the splendor through the dim,
His vision so attendeth him,
Whate'er he views by others shown,
His revelation bides his own.

REVEALED

NOW, on a sudden, I know it, the secret, the
secret of life.
Why, the very green of the grass in the fields with
betrayal is rife!
The whirr of the grasshopper by the wayside pro-
claims it to all;
'T is unrolled as a scroll to all eyes in the curve of
the waterfall.
But, for me, I can only wonder at mortals, — the
secret out;
For they see, hear, taste, smell, feel not what Heaven
reveals all about.

KEARSARGE

THIS morning on my eastward road
Kearsarge's top a diamond glowed.
At noon on its ice-planed ridge I lie,
Facing the neighbor clouds on high ;
My back is warmed by the sun-bathed stone, —
A child of earth myself I own,
And yet within for flight endowed,
To float, a brother to the cloud.
An eagle swims the gulf abreast,
Eyeing askance his unknown guest.
O Eagle, I wonder if thou art
Nearer than I to the mountain's heart ;
Canst better the hidden meaning guess
Of its vast and cavernous silences ;
The burden of its midnight moan,
The plaint of the rain on its breast of stone,
Or the Cause whereto its trumpet-call
Summons the world to fight or fall.

But hither though we twain may come,
Neither here can build his home.
Thine is the tree-top half-way down,
And mine in the lowland, the far-off town.
Thy tongue I know not, thou knowst not mine ;
We dimly interpret by sound and sign ;

64

KEARSARGE

Then how shall either the secret reach
Of the mountain's formless and primal speech?
Yet all-prevailing is love that abides;
Not wholly its meaning the mountain hides
From thee in thy patient, circling flight,
Nor me outstretched on its sailing height.
For what we lack it behooves us wait;
And what we have learned, with hearts elate,
Yet awed by the mountain's mighty sway,
To ponder, understand, and obey.

BABYHOOD

THE baby learns by bumps and bruises,
    Else could he never learn at all.
Now, who can tell but this the use is
    Of earthly life to great and small?

Our world was haply made to fail in,
    The place to learn how not to do;
To blunder, stumble, ache, and wail in,
    Till out of false we learn the true.

MORROW-SONGS

MEDIO TUTISSIMUS IBIS

THEY bade me take the middle course
And shun a palsied eld's remorse;
Betimes to rise and eke to bed,
Look not on wine or lips when red,
In food and drink, in speech and dress,
Avoiding spareness and excess;
Ever as Wisdom's final touch
To take the rule of " Not too much."

By this rule have I lived my life,
Free from ambition, joy, or strife;
And now, when fourscore years are done,
I strike the balance, and have won
From all, head, heart, and hand have brought
In fourscore years of living — naught.
Better one pang of love's defeat,
One mad thought hammered at white heat,
One dash to gain a hopeless goal,
Than Life triumphant over Soul.

THE TRIUMPH OF TOIL

O GOLDEN Dreams that I loved and toiled
but to feed,
This is the triumph of toil, that no longer I heed
You, whom I toiled for by day to possess at night,
But find night and day in toil my only delight.

THE PLAYER

YON man with hollow cheeks and eyes of fire,
And hair upstarting, as he smites the lyre;
The message it so wrings him to convey,
That music, dar'st thou hear and call it *play?*

SONG-LULL

WHY are our poets silent? Is it in
The utter wanhope of this devil's-din,
Which stuns men into deafness? Do not fear!
That low-born jangle never meets their ear.
It is because too near sweeps roaring by
The flaming robe of giant Destiny.

THE TIME-SERVER

HE serves the Time with knuckle and nod,
And Time, who is a generous god,
Gives him all that heart can desire,
Except, it may be, prophetic fire.

GENIUS

AT last the doom of genius is made plain; —
Not heavenly-fed the beacon we behold,
Which turns the dusk of earthly life to gold,
But stealing sustenance from heart and brain.
No marvel if the streaming Pharos drain
The strength that lifts it, and with manifold
Disaster crashing fall, its years half told,
A fume bat-winged with every shape of pain.

Twin-born its wreck and splendor. — Oh! rejoice
That we have learned its secret, and no more
May cheapen with blind insult or defence
Its godlike doom, wherein was writ no choice
And no escape. The dead vain tears deplore;
The living claim love's tardy penitence.

FERTILITY

A MONTH devoid of song, but strown
With toil and pain and anxious care,—
The cumbering draff through which alone
Song's fragrant blossoms leap to air.

GUIDED

MUSE, we have rowed on glassy streams,
Poised 'twixt the skies of truth and dreams;
You, at the tiller, lolled to trail
A water-lily o'er the rail;
I, drunken with your beauty's wine,
Recked only of its breath divine,
Nor dreamed what high up-clashing seas
Should follow swift that love-lapped ease.

On those white surges tost and whirled,
An atom in a strangling world,
Without a star, without a ray,
We drove through wrecks of night and day,
You guiding still our dizzy flight,
I at your feet benumbed with fright,
Till suddenly you seized my hand,
And lo! we were in peace at land.

MORROW-SONGS

On this Enchanted Isle our stay
Or long or short is yours to say.
Here all about us rolls the sea,
Its terror now a part of me,
To heighten joys like these I know,
Reclining on your breast of snow,
Yet to assure by sea or land
My welfare at your guiding hand.

THE WAY STATION

TWELVE times a day the train whirls by,
 Four times my humble name it heeds;
I live not in the traveler's eye
 More than the rail o'er which he speeds.

From the great city forward borne
 To the great city of his quest,
Awake or slumbering, night or morn,
 He recks not of my toil or rest.

Yet, but for me, the giant mart
 Would melt like drifted smoke of trains;
Its very stones are all my part,
 And mine its conquering hands and brains.

CULTURE

BEAUTY,—ah! yes, but first let Justice be
    done in the earth,
  Justice, which brings Heaven down from the
    barren stars to the ground,
Here to be dwelt-in of men — Heaven's only mean-
    ing and worth ;
  And in Heaven or this our Hell, think you, shall
    Beauty be found ?

Nay, dream not of Heaven below ; the utmost that
    earth can give,
  The highest of human life, the perfectest Golden
    Age,
Will not be Heaven brought down, where men
    shall as angels live,
  But Purgatory, where still we shall climb from
    stage to stage.

• BEFORE DAWN

BECAUSE I spurned the manikin men name
  The Ineffable Name, they shrieked and stopped
    their ears.
  But taunts of " Atheist " lend my death no fears ;

MORROW-SONGS

My dread is all lest I, as meet for blame,
Reared too my idol when I durst proclaim :
    Exalt we Plato's thought, the Christ's warm
        tears,
    And Cæsar's throne above heaven's topmost
        spheres,
The Infinite outsoars them still the same.

Silence had holier been ; I see it now,
    Lying 'twixt night and what shall follow night.
Better to stand with bare and open brow
    Confessing never can our human sight
Attain thy garment's hem ; yea, to avow
    Earth's dark not even the nadir of thy light.

DUST

SATANIC Science, to reveal
    A speck of dust the snowflake's core !
Well, bravo, dust ! If you could steal
    Angelic plumes, we 'll mope no more.

TWO POETS

HE had a straight Greek brow, which sculptors
  loved,
  And clear and pure his classic measures rang.
Men hailed him bard by all the gods approved,
  And snowy maids his star-cold numbers sang.

Look now on this face. Mark the bulging brow,
  The shapeless mouth, the torn and twisted ear,
The seams of riot. Nay, who marks them now?
  He fired men's hearts to win our Golden Year.

www.ingramcontent.com/pod-product-compliance
Lightning Source LLC
Chambersburg PA
CBHW021427090426
42742CB00009B/1293